Marian

Prayers and Devotions

A Redemptorist Pastoral Publication
Compiled by Brother Daniel Korn, C.Ss.R.

Liguori

ONE LIGUORI DRIVE
LIGUORI MO 63057-9999

Imprimi Potest:
Richard Thibodeau, C.Ss.R.
Provincial, Denver Province
The Redemptorists

Imprimatur:
Most Reverend Michael J. Sheridan
Auxiliary Bishop, Archdiocese of St. Louis

ISBN 0-7648-0605-5
Library of Congress Catalog Card Number: 98-68828

© 2000, Liguori Publications
Printed in the United States of America
04 03 02 01 00   5 4 3 2 1

To order, call 1-800-325-9521
http://www.liguori.org

Cover image, Mother of God, reprinted with permission of Conciliar Press. *www.conciliarpress.com*
Cover design by Wendy Barnes

Contents

Prayers for Liturgical Feasts of the Blessed Virgin Mary 33

Devotion to the Blessed Virgin Mary 41

Prayers to the Blessed Virgin Mary 75

Hymns 78

Queen of Heaven 80

We Turn to You for Protection

History of Devotion to the Blessed Virgin Mary

The Blessed Virgin Mary has always held a very special place of devotion in the life of Roman Catholics. This devotion can be traced back to the earliest times of the Church. One of the oldest prayers to the Mother of God is found on a Greek papyrus (c. A.D. 300): "We turn to you for protection, holy Mother of God" (*Sub tuum praesidium*). Another example is an Ethiopic hymn to our Lady (c. 400).

Saint Bernard of Clairvaux is famous for his devotion to Mary and for his writings on the place of Mary in the life of the Church. Tradition credits him with popularizing the familiar prayer, the *Memorare*. Saint Alphonsus Liguori, known for his devotion to Mary, would often preach and write on his favorite theme: "No one truly devoted to Mary is lost." His famous book *The Glories of Mary* details how those who have devotion to Mary are led to the redemptive love of Jesus Christ. Saint Louis Marie de Montfort's *True Devotion to the Blessed Virgin Mary* continues to be a classic guide to living a Marian spirituality.

In his book *Mysteries of Mary,* Father Bernard Häring, a well-known Redemptorist theologian, captures the ways in which Mary models perfect discipleship for us, drawing on scriptural references from the Annunciation through Pentecost.

As part of *The Dogmatic Constitution on the Church,* the Second Vatican Council included an eighth chapter called "The Role of the Blessed Virgin Mary, Mother of God, in the Mystery of Christ and the Church." This chapter of the document presents the function of the Blessed Virgin in God's plan of salvation, her relationship to the Church, her role as Mother of the Lord, and her example to us of discipleship. She is a sign of hope and comfort for the whole Church.

Devoutly meditating on her and contemplating her in the light of the Word made flesh, the Church reverently penetrates more deeply into the great mystery of the Incarnation and becomes more and more like [Jesus Christ]. The Church, therefore in her apostolic work too, rightly looks to her who gave birth to Christ, who was conceived of the Holy Spirit and born of a virgin in order that through the Church he could be born and increase in the hearts of the faithful. In her life, the Virgin has been a model of that motherly love with which all who join in the Church's apostolic mission for the regeneration of mankind should be animated.

#65

The *Catechism of the Catholic Church* states,

Mary is the perfect *Orans (pray-er),* a figure of the Church. When we pray to her, we are adhering with her to the plan of the Father, who sends his Son to save [us]. Like the beloved disciple we welcome Jesus' mother into our homes, for she has become the mother of all the living. We can pray with and

to her. The prayer of the Church is sustained by the prayer of Mary and united with it in hope.
#2679

The purpose of this prayer book is to help people in their devotion to the Mother of the Lord. However, true devotion to Mary is not measured by the number of prayers we say. Imitating Mary in our daily lives is the heart of devotion. True devotion to Mary always leads us to a greater desire to know Jesus Christ. Not much is written in the Scriptures about Mary, but what little is written about her is powerful in example. The silence of Mary speaks volumes. Luke tells us that "Mary treasured all these words and pondered them in her heart." Like Mary, we must learn the ways of silence before God. Her simple *fiat*—"Be it done to me as you say"—contains the secret of living a life of discipleship and surrender.

The *Decree on the Apostolate of Lay People* tells us

Perfect model of this apostolic spiritual life is the Blessed Virgin Mary, Queen of Apostles.

While on earth her life was like that of any other, filled with labors and the cares of the home; always, however, she remained intimately united to her Son and cooperated in an entirely unique way in the Savior's work. And now, assumed into heaven, "her motherly love keeps her attentive to her Son's brothers [and sisters], still on pilgrimage amid the dangers and difficulties of life, until they arrive at the happiness of the fatherland." Everyone should have a genuine devotion to her and entrust [their] life to her motherly care.

#4

On the inside back cover of this prayer book is a picture of Our Lady of Good Counsel. Saint Alphonsus always had a picture of her on his desk. He placed his many apostolic efforts into her powerful hands. Following his example, we entrust ourselves to the Mother of the Savior.

May this book of prayers lead you closer to Jesus Christ through the example of Mary, his mother and ours.

Ancient Prayers to Mary

We Turn to You for Protection (Sub Tuum Praesidium)

We turn to you for protection, holy Mother of God. Listen to our prayers, and help us in our needs. Save us from every danger, glorious and blessed Virgin Mary.

Hail, Holy Mother

Hail, Holy Mother of God, virgin full of grace, the Lord is with you. Blessed are you among women, and blessed is the fruit of your holy womb. For you have given birth to our Savior and Deliverer, Jesus the Christ. Amen

Prayer of Saint Ephrem

Immaculate and pure Virgin Mary, Mother of God, queen of the universe, you are above all the saints, the hope of the patriarchs and the joy of the saints.

Through you we have been reconciled with God. You are the only advocate of sinners and the safe refuge of those who sail the sea of life.

You are the consolation of the world, the ransom of captives, the joy of the sick, the comfort of the afflicted, the refuge and the salvation of the whole world.

Liturgical Prayers

It has long been the practice in the Catholic Church that Saturday is a special day set aside to honor Mary. One such practice is the Office of the Blessed Virgin Mary, modeled on the Liturgy of the Hours. The following Morning and Evening Prayer for Saturdays and Marian feast days are suggested for your prayer.

Liturgy of the Hours in Honor of the Blessed Virgin Mary for Saturday

Morning Prayer

V. God, come to my assistance,
R. Lord, make haste to help me.
V. Glory to the Father, the Son, and the Holy Spirit,
R. Both now and forever. Amen

HYMN (OPTIONAL. SEE PAGES 78-80.)

PSALM 92

Antiphon: Rejoice Virgin Mary, for the Lord is with you.

It is good to give thanks to the Lord,
to sing praise to your name, O Most High,
to proclaim your grace in the morning,
to declare your faithfulness at night,
accompanied by music from the lyre
and the melody of lute and harp.

For you make me glad with your deeds, O Lord,
and I sing for joy at the work of your hands.
How great are your works,
O Lord, how deep your thoughts!

The senseless will not know,
nor will the stupid understand them.
For though the wicked prosper
and evildoers flourish like grass,
they are doomed to vanish for good.
But you, O Lord, are exalted forever.

Time will come when your enemies will perish,
evildoers will be scattered.

You have made me stronger than the wild ox;
you have poured fresh oil on me.
I look down on my enemies;
I take for granted their doom.

The virtuous will flourish like palm trees,
they will thrive like the cedars of Lebanon.
Planted in the house of the Lord,
they will prosper in the courts of our God.

In old age they will still bear fruit
they will stay fresh and green,
to proclaim that the Lord is upright,
"He is my Rock," they say, "he never fails."

Glory to the Father, the Son, and the Holy Spirit,
both now and forever. Amen

ANTIPHON

SCRIPTURE READING: REVELATION 12:1

A great sign appeared in heaven: a woman, clothed with the sun, with the moon under her feet and a crown of twelve stars on her head.

SILENT REFLECTION

CANTICLE OF ZECHARIAH
(LUKE 1:68-79)

Blessed be the Lord God of Israel, for he has looked favorably on his people and redeemed them.

He has raised up a mighty Savior for us in the house of his servant David, as he spoke through the mouth of his holy prophets from of old, that we would be saved from our enemies and from the hand of all who hate us.

Thus he has shown the mercy promised to our ancestors, and has remembered his holy covenant, the oath that he swore to our ancestor Abraham, to grant us that we, being rescued from the hands of our enemies, might serve him without fear, in holiness and righteousness before him all our days.

And you, child, will be called the prophet of the Most High; for you will go before the Lord to prepare his ways, to give knowledge of salvation to his people by the forgiveness of their sins.

By the tender mercy of our God, the dawn from on high will break upon us, to give light to those who sit in darkness and in the shadow of death, to guide our feet into the way of peace.

Glory to the Father, the Son, and the Holy Spirit, both now and forever. Amen

PRAYERS OF INTERCESSION

We give glory to our Lord Jesus Christ, who chose Mary for his mother. We gather our petitions and offer them to the Blessed Virgin Mary, that she may intercede to her son Jesus in our behalf. *(Here make your intentions.)*

THE LORD'S PRAYER

Our Father, who art in heaven, hallowed be thy name. Thy kingdom come, thy will be done on earth as it is in heaven. Give us this day our daily bread, and forgive us our trespasses, as we forgive those who trespass against us. And lead us not into temptation, but deliver us from evil. (For the kingdom, the power, and the glory are yours, now and forever.) Amen

Closing Prayer

Almighty God, you chose Mary of Nazareth to be the Mother of your Son, our Lord Jesus Christ. May our devotion in her honor be pleasing to you.

We ask this through our Lord Jesus Christ, your Son, who lives and reigns with you and the Holy Spirit, one God, forever and ever. Amen

Evening Prayer

V. God, come to my assistance,
R. Lord, make haste to help me.
V. Glory to the Father, the Son, and the Holy Spirit,
R. Both now and forever. Amen

Hymn (Optional. See pages 78-80.)

Psalm 130

Antiphon: Beautiful and wonderful things are said about you, Holy Virgin Mary.

Out of the depths I cry to you, O Lord,
O Lord, hear my voice!
Let your ears pay attention
to the voice of my supplication.

If you should mark our evil,
O Lord, who could stand?
But with you is forgiveness,
and for that you are revered.

I waited for the Lord, my soul waits,
and I put my hope in his word.
My soul expected the Lord
more than watchmen the dawn.

O Israel, hope in the Lord,
for with him is unfailing love
and with him full deliverance.
He will deliver Israel
from all its sins.

Glory to the Father, the Son, and the Holy Spirit,
both now and forever. Amen

ANTIPHON

May God ensure your everlasting glory, and may he reward and bless you for you have risked your life when your race was humiliated. You chose instead to do the best before God in order to prevent our downfall. And all the people said, "Amen! Amen!"

SILENT REFLECTION

CANTICLE OF MARY
(LUKE 1:46-55)

My soul magnifies the Lord,
and my spirit rejoices in God my Savior,
for he has looked with favor on the lowliness of
    his servant.

Surely, from now on all generations will call me
    blessed;
for the Mighty One has done great things for me,
and holy is his name.

His mercy is for those who fear him
from generation to generation.
He has shown strength with his arm;

he has scattered the proud in the thoughts of their
   hearts.

He has brought down the powerful from their
   thrones,
and lifted up the lowly;
he has filled the hungry with good things,
and sent the rich away empty.

He has helped his servant Israel,
in remembrance of his mercy,
according to the promise he made to our ancestors,
to Abraham and to his descendants forever.

Glory to the Father, the Son, and the Holy Spirit,
both now and forever. Amen

PRAYERS OF INTERCESSION

We give glory to our Lord Jesus Christ, who chose
Mary for his mother. We gather our petitions and
offer them to the Blessed Virgin Mary, that she may
intercede to her son Jesus in our behalf. *(Here make
your intentions.)*

THE LORD'S PRAYER (SEE PAGE 18.)

Lord our God, you created the Virgin Mary as a model for all who hear the word of God and keep it. Open our hearts to receive the Word with joy. May the Holy Spirit make us a worthy dwelling place for your Word of salvation.

We ask this through our Lord Jesus Christ, your Son, who lives and reigns with you and the Holy Spirit, one God, forever and ever. Amen

Liturgy of the Hours
For Special Feast Days of the
Blessed Virgin Mary

Morning Prayer

V. God, come to my assistance,
R. Lord, make haste to help me.
V. Glory to the Father, the Son, and the Holy Spirit,
R. Both now and forever. Amen

HYMN (OPTIONAL. SEE PAGES 78-80.)

PSALM 119:41-50

Antiphon: Let us rejoice in the Lord as we celebrate this feast in honor of the Blessed Virgin Mary.

Give me your unfailing love, O Lord,
your salvation as you have promised.

Strengthened by my trust in your word,
I can answer my enemy's reproach.

Take not the word of truth from my mouth,
for I would also lose my hope in your word.

May I always keep your word forever and ever;
I shall walk in freedom, having sought out your
laws.

I will proclaim your word before kings,
and I will not be confused or ashamed.

For I delight in your word, which I fear.
I will lift up my hands to you,
and meditate on your commandments.

Remember your word to your servant,
your word which has given me hope.

My consolation in suffering is this:
that your promise renews my life.

Glory to the Father, the Son, and the Holy Spirit,
both now and forever. Amen

ANTIPHON

PSALM 9:2-3,10-12

Antiphon: Come, let us give worship to Christ, the
Son of Mary.

Let my heart give thanks to the Lord,
I yearn to proclaim your marvelous deeds,
and rejoice and exult in you,
and sing praise to your name, O Most High.

The Lord is a rampart for the oppressed,
a refuge in times of distress.

Those who cherish your name, O Lord,
can rely on you,
for you have never forsaken those who look to you.

Sing praises to the Lord enthroned in Zion,
proclaim his deeds among the nations.

Glory to the Father, the Son, and the Holy Spirit, both now and forever. Amen

ANTIPHON

SCRIPTURE READING: SONG OF SONGS 6:9-10

My dove, my perfect one,
is unique, the only daughter
and favorite of her mother.

Who is this coming like the dawn,
fair as the moon, bright as the sun,
majestic as bannered troops?

OR TITUS 2:11-13

For God our Savior has revealed his loving plan to all, teaching us to reject an irreligious way of life and worldly greed, and to live in this world as responsible persons, upright and serving God, while we await our blessed hope—the glorious manifestation of our great God and Savior Christ Jesus.

OR HEBREWS 1:1-2

God has spoken in the past to our fathers through the prophets, in many different ways, although never completely; but in our times he has spoken definitively to us through his Son.

SILENT REFLECTION

CANTICLE OF ZECHARIAH (SEE PAGE 17.)

PRAYERS OF INTERCESSION

We give glory to our Lord Jesus Christ, who chose Mary for his mother. We gather our petitions and offer them to the Blessed Virgin Mary, that she may intercede to her son Jesus in our behalf. *(Here make your intentions.)*

THE LORD'S PRAYER (SEE PAGE 18.)

CLOSING PRAYER

Loving God our Father, look upon the Virgin Mary whose life on earth was governed by a spirit of acceptance. Give to us your children the gift of prayerful surrender that marked her life.

We ask this through our Lord Jesus Christ, your Son, who lives and reigns with you and the Holy Spirit, one God, forever and ever. Amen

Evening Prayer

V. God, come to my assistance,
R. Lord, make haste to help me.
V. Glory to the Father, the Son, and the Holy Spirit,
R. Both now and forever. Amen

HYMN (OPTIONAL. SEE PAGES 78-80.)

PSALM 131
Antiphon: Rejoice Mary, Mother of the Lord.

O Lord, my heart is not proud
nor do I have arrogant eyes.
I am not engrossed in ambitious matters,
nor in things too great for me.

I have quieted and stilled my soul
like a weaned child on its mother's lap;
like a contented child is my soul.
Hope in the Lord, O Israel,
now and forever.

Glory to the Father, the Son, and the Holy Spirit,
both now and forever. Amen

ANTIPHON

PSALM 132:1-10
Antiphon: Mary, you are blessed by the Lord our
God.

Remember David, O Lord, and all his readiness,
how he swore an oath to the Lord,
to the Mighty One of Jacob.

"I will not enter my house
nor get into my bed,
I will give no sleep to my eyes,
no slumber to my eyelids,
until I find a place for the Lord,
a dwelling for the Mighty One of Jacob."

Then came the news, "The Ark is in Ephrathah,
we found it in the fields of Jaar."
Let us go to where he dwells
and worship at his footstool!

Arise, O Lord, and come to your rest,
you and the ark of your might.

May your priests be arrayed as for a triumphing;
may your faithful ones shout in gladness.

For the sake of your servant, David,
do not turn away the face of your anointed.

Glory to the Father, the Son, and the Holy Spirit,
both now and forever. Amen

ANTIPHON

SCRIPTURE READING: ISAIAH 61:10
I rejoice greatly in Yahweh, my soul exults for joy
in my God, for he has clothed me in the garments
of his salvation, he has covered me with the robe of
his righteousness, like a bridegroom wearing a gar-
land, like a bride adorned with jewels.

OR GALATIANS 4:4-5

When the fullness of time came, God sent his Son. He came born of woman and subject to the Law, in order to redeem the subjects of the Law, that we may be given our full rights as sons and daughters of God.

OR ZECHARIAH 9:9

Rejoice greatly, daughter of Zion! Shout for joy, daughter of Jerusalem! For your king is coming, just and victorious, humble and riding on a donkey, on a colt, the foal of a donkey.

SILENT REFLECTION

CANTICLE OF MARY (SEE PAGE 21.)

PRAYERS OF INTERCESSION

We give glory to our Lord Jesus Christ, who chose Mary for his mother. We gather our petitions and offer them to the Blessed Virgin Mary, that she may intercede to her son Jesus in our behalf. *(Here make your intentions.)*

THE LORD'S PRAYER (SEE PAGE 18.)

CLOSING PRAYER

God of eternal glory, your Word, Jesus Christ, became flesh in the womb of Mary. Because of this the whole world is filled with joy. Free us from our selfishness and remove the sadness that extinguishes your Spirit, and make us worthy to sit at the table of your kingdom, where you nourish us with the bread of joy. We ask this through our Lord Jesus Christ, your Son, who lives and reigns with you and the Holy Spirit, one God, forever and ever. Amen

Prayers for Liturgical Feasts of the Blessed Virgin Mary

❦

Solemnity of the Blessed Virgin Mary, Mother of God

(January 1)

Blessed Virgin Mary, today we celebrate the oldest feast in your honor. We give thanks to God for choosing you to be the mother of Jesus. You are blessed, Virgin Mary, for the Lord is truly with you. Hear us as we call upon you, our mother. Amen

Feast of Our Lady of Lourdes

(February 11)

Blessed Virgin Mary, we celebrate the feast of your appearances to Bernadette at Lourdes. We give honor to you, Immaculate Virgin, and we honor the grace of your Immaculate Conception. The waters of Lourdes are blessed with the healing mercy of your son, Jesus. Join your prayers with ours as we implore the mercy of God in our lives. Amen

Solemnity of the Annunciation of the Lord

(March 25)

Blessed Virgin Mary, on this day we give thanks to the Holy Trinity for choosing you to be the mother of our Savior, Jesus Christ. By your prayers, help us to hear the Word of God and respond with generous hearts to the message of the gospel. May we live our lives in humble service to our sisters and brothers who are most in need. Amen

Feast of the Visitation of the Blessed Virgin Mary

(May 31)

Blessed Virgin Mary, in your visit to your cousin Elizabeth, you show us an example of charity toward our neighbor. Pray for us that we might be filled with the same Holy Spirit that filled you and Elizabeth, so that we might be messengers of love and mercy to those we meet on our journey of life. Amen

Memorial of the Immaculate Heart of Mary

(Saturday following the Second Sunday after Pentecost)

Blessed Virgin Mary, God the Father prepared your heart to be a special dwelling place for the Holy Spirit. Pray for us that we may open our hearts to the workings of the Holy Spirit. Form our hearts into Christ-like temples of mercy and love. May we be instruments of peace and joy. Amen

Memorial of Our Lady of Mount Carmel

(July 16)

Blessed Virgin Mary, you are the glorious flower of Mount Carmel and the joy of the Christian people. Cover us with the mantle of your motherly love and help us to live the gospel of your son. Protect us from all danger and sickness. Guide us in this life to walk in humility and love. Amen

Feast of the Dedication of Saint Mary Major

(August 5)

Blessed Virgin Mary, we honor you as Mother of Jesus our Savior. You are the temple of the Holy Spirit. In you dwelt the Word of God, Jesus the Lord. Pray for us, Mary, that we may become a worthy dwelling place of the Holy Spirit. Amen

Solemnity of the Assumption of the Blessed Virgin Mary

(August 15)

Blessed Virgin Mary, God bestowed special graces upon you that you might be the mother of his Son. The privilege of your Assumption gives hope to us who daily strive to live the gospel. Pray with us that we may reflect your example of holiness. May we one day come to share in the Resurrection of Jesus, the Lord. Amen

Memorial of the Queenship of the Blessed Virgin Mary

(August 22)

Blessed Virgin Mary, you are our mother and queen. We honor you for your humility and faithfulness. As Mother of the Christ, you walked in faith as you witnessed the saving work of Jesus, your son. Inspire us to live our lives in faithful service to the gospel. Amen

Feast of the Birth of the Blessed Virgin Mary

(September 8)

Blessed Virgin Mary, at your birth the patriarchs and prophets rejoiced, for you announced the coming of our salvation. We celebrate your birth and ask your help in our daily lives. In a world filled with violence, fear, and anxiety, help us to be examples of living in gospel joy. Amen

Memorial of Our Lady of Sorrows

(September 15)

Blessed Virgin Mary, you watched in anguish as your son died on the cross for our salvation. Through your sufferings, may the whole Church be ever mindful of the passion of Jesus. By your prayers, may our eyes be opened to the sufferings of those around us. Following your example, may we be people of compassion and love. Amen

Memorial of Our Lady of the Rosary

(October 7)

Blessed Virgin Mary, the mysteries of the rosary lead us to meditate on the life of Jesus, the Redeemer. May our meditation on the mysteries of our salvation bring us to live the life of Christ in the world. May we imitate what these holy mysteries contain and receive what they promise. Amen

Memorial of the Presentation of the Blessed Virgin Mary

(November 21)

Blessed Virgin Mary, today we remember and celebrate your dedication to the service of the Lord. Assist us with your prayers that we live more fully the call of our baptism and confirmation. Amen

Solemnity of the Immaculate Conception

(December 8)

Blessed Virgin Mary, the feast of your Immaculate Conception brings joy to the Church. May your motherly concern for us keep our lives free from the evil of sin. May we imitate your life of humble faith and service. Amen

Feast of Our Lady of Guadalupe

(December 12)

Blessed Virgin Mary, the people of the Americas are filled with joy, for your motherly love was revealed at Tepeyac. You are the great sign that appeared in the sky, a woman clothed with the sun, with the moon under her feet, and her head crowned with twelve stars. Assist us with your prayers that we may love each other as sisters and brothers of your Son, Jesus Christ. Amen

Devotion to the Blessed Virgin Mary

✦

The Hail Mary

Hail Mary, full of grace, the Lord is with you. Blessed are you among women, and blessed is the fruit of your womb, Jesus.

Holy Mary, Mother of God, pray for us sinners, now and at the hour of our death. Amen

Devotion of the Hail Mary by Saint Alphonsus Liguori

This angelic salutation is most pleasing to the Blessed Virgin Mary. Whenever she hears it, the remembrance of the joy of Gabriel's announcement is renewed in her. Because of this we should often salute her with "Hail Mary."

There are six reasons to practice this devotion of reciting the Hail Mary. First, we can pray the Hail Mary three times on rising from our sleep and on going to bed in the evening. We may add to these Hail Marys the invocation: *Mary, by your holy and Immaculate Conception, make my body pure and my soul holy.*

Second, we can say the Angelus morning, noon, and evening with the usual three Hail Marys. Third, we can honor the Mother of God with a Hail Mary every time we look at the clock. Fourth, in going in and out of our homes we can say the Hail Mary for her protection over us. Fifth, whenever we see a picture or statue of our Lady, we can say the Hail Mary. For this purpose, if we can, we should have a picture of our Lady in our home. Sixth, we can acquire the habit of beginning and ending our daily projects with a Hail Mary.

Dedication to the Blessed Virgin Mary

Most holy Virgin Mary, Mother of God, I_____, although unworthy to be your servant, yet moved by your wonderful compassion and by my desire to serve you, now choose you, in the presence of my guardian angel and of the whole heavenly court, as my advocate and mother. I resolve always to love and serve you for the future and to do whatever I can to lead others to love and serve you. I ask you, Mother of God, by the blood which your son shed for me, to receive me as your servant. Assist me in all my thoughts, words, and actions in every moment of my life, so that every step I take and every breath I breathe may be directed to the glory of God. Through your powerful intercession, may I turn from sin and never offend Jesus. May my life give glory and honor to him. With you, may I praise him forever in heaven. My Mother Mary, I recommend my soul to you now and at the hour of my death. Amen

Feasc Day Meditations

The Presentation of Jesus in the Temple
(February 2)

When the time had come in which, according to the law, Mary was to be purified in the Temple and to present Jesus to the Eternal Father, she, accompanied by Saint Joseph, directed her steps toward Jerusalem. Joseph took two turtledoves, which were to be offered, and Mary took her beloved Infant. She took the Divine Lamb to offer it to God, as a token of the great sacrifice which he would one day accomplish on the cross.

My God, I also unite my sacrifice to that of Mary: I offer your Incarnate Son; and by His merits I beseech you to grant me your grace. I do not deserve it; but Jesus sacrificed himself to you to obtain it for me. For the love of Jesus, then, have mercy on me.

The Annunciation
(March 25)

When God was pleased to send his Son on earth, that by becoming man he might redeem lost man, he chose him a Virgin Mother, who, among all virgins, was the most pure, the most holy, and the most humble. While Mary was in her poor dwelling, beseeching God to send the promised Redeemer, an angel stood before her and saluted her, saying, "Hail, full of grace; the Lord is with you; blessed are you among women." And what was the conduct of this humble Virgin when she heard so honorable a salutation? She was not elated, but was silent and troubled, considering herself indeed unworthy of such praises: "She was troubled at his saying." O Mary, you are so humble, and I am so filled with pride; obtain for me holy humility.

The Visitation
(May 31)

Mary set out from Nazareth to go to the city of Judea, in which Saint Elizabeth resided; a distance of seventy miles, or at least seven days' journey. The holy and tender Virgin hastened her steps, as Saint Luke tells us: "Mary, rising up in those days, went into the hill country with haste." Tell us, O holy Lady, why did you undertake so long and arduous a journey, and why did you hasten? "I went," she replies, "to exercise my office of charity: I went to console a family." Since, O great Mother of God, your office is to console and dispense graces to souls, be graciously pleased also to visit and console my soul. Your visit sanctified the house of Elizabeth: come, O Mary, and sanctify me also.

The Assumption
(August 15)

Mary died; but how did she die? She died entirely detached from all created things; she died consumed by that Divine love which during her whole life had always inflamed her most holy heart. O holy Mother, you have already left the earth; do not forget us miserable pilgrims who remain in this valley of tears, struggling against so many enemies who wish to drag us to hell. Ah, by the merits of your precious death be graciously pleased to obtain for us detachment from earthly things, the forgiveness of our sins, love of God, and holy perseverance; and when the hour of death arrives, help us from heaven with your prayers, and obtain for us that we may kiss your feet in Paradise.

The Birth of Mary
(September 8)

Before the birth of Mary, the world was lost in the darkness of sin. "Mary was born, and the dawn arose," says a holy father. Of Mary it had already been said, "Who is she that comes forth as the morning rising?" As the earth rejoices when the dawn appears, because it is the precursor of the sun, so also when Mary was born the whole world rejoiced, because she was the precursor of Jesus Christ, the Sun of Justice, who being made her son, came to save us by his death. The Church sings, "Your nativity, O Virgin Mother of God, announced joy to the whole world; for from you arose the Sun of Justice, who has given us life eternal." So that when Mary was born, our remedy, our consolation, and our salvation came into the world; for through Mary we received our Savior.

The Presentation of Mary
(November 21)

Mary had hardly attained the age of three years when she entreated her holy parents to take her to the Temple, according to the promise which they had made. The appointed day having arrived, the immaculate young Virgin left Nazareth with Saint Joachim and Saint Anne; a choir of angels also accompanied that holy child, who was destined to become the Mother of their Creator. "Go," says Saint Germanus, "go, O Blessed Virgin, to the house of the Lord, to await the coming of the Holy Ghost, who will make you the Mother of the Eternal Word."

The Immaculate Conception
(December 8)

It was indeed becoming that the three Divine Persons should preserve Mary from original sin. It was becoming that the Father should do so, because Mary was his first-born daughter. As Jesus was the first-born of God, "the first-born of every creature," so also was Mary, the destined Mother of God, always considered by him as his first-born daughter by adoption, and therefore he always possessed her by his grace: "The Lord possessed me in the beginning of his ways." For the honor, therefore, of his Son, it was becoming that the Father should preserve his Mother from every stain of sin. It was also becoming that he should do so, because he destined this his daughter to crush the head of the infernal serpent. "She shall crush thy head." How, then, could he permit that she should first be the slave of this infernal serpent? Moreover, Mary was also destined to become the advocate of sinners; therefore it was also becoming that God should preserve her from sin.

It is impossible for a child of Mary, who is faithful in honoring and recommending themselves to her, to be lost.

Adapted from
The Glories of Mary,
by Saint Alphonsus Liguori

Acclamations

Mary and Christ Prayer

Mary the dawn, Christ the glorious day;
Mary the gate, Christ the heavenly way.
Mary the root, Christ the holy vine;
Mary the grape, Christ the sacred wine.
Mary the wheat, Christ the living bread;
Mary the stem, Christ the rose blood-red.
Mary the font, Christ the healing flood;
Mary the chalice, Christ the saving blood.
Mary the temple, Christ the temple's Lord;
Mary the shrine, Christ the God adored.
Mary the beacon, Christ the haven's rest;
Mary the mirror, Christ the vision blest.
Mary the Mother, Christ the Mother's Son;
Glory and praise while endless ages run.

Loving Mother of the Redeemer

Loving Mother of the Redeemer, gate of heaven, star of the sea, assist your people who have fallen but strive to rise again. You joyfully bore Christ our Savior to the whole world and remained a virgin as before. You who received the angel's joyful greeting, look with love and kindness on us your children. Amen

Help of the Helpless

Holy Virgin Mary, you are the help of the helpless, you are the strength of the fearful, you are the consolation of the sorrowful. Pray for your people, help the clergy, intercede for all consecrated women and men; may all who honor you experience the powerful help of your assistance. Amen

Novenas to the Blessed Virgin Mary

◦✦◦

Novena in Honor of Mother of Perpetual Help

(If the novena is prayed in common, start with a hymn in honor of Mary from your own resources or one from pages 78-80.)

Mother of Perpetual Help, you have been blessed and favored by God. You became not only the Mother of the Redeemer but the Mother of the Redeemed as well. We come to you today as your loving children. Watch over us and take care of us. As you held the child Jesus in your loving arms, so take us in your arms. Be a mother ready at every moment to help us, for God who is mighty has done great things for you, and God's mercy is from age to age on those who love God. Our greatest fear is that, in time of temptation, we may fail to call out to you and become lost children. Intercede for us, dear Mother, in obtaining pardon for our sins, love for Jesus, final perseverance, and the grace always to call upon you, Mother of Perpetual Help.

Mother of Perpetual Help, pray for us.

Proclamation of Praise in Honor of Mary

Glorious and wonderful things are said about you, our Virgin Mary. You are the glory and joy of the Christian people. You are the defender of the poor and rejected. You are the safe refuge of the persecuted and a mother ever ready to help us. Surround us with the radiance of your loving protection, and keep us safe from all that would harm us, glorious and powerful Mother of the Redeemer.

Scripture Reading: Luke 2:33-35

His father and mother wondered at what was said about the child. Simeon blessed them and said to Mary, his mother, "See him; he will be for the rise or fall of the multitudes of Israel. He shall stand as a sign of contradiction, while a sword will pierce your own soul. Then the secret thoughts of many may be brought to light."

(Instead of the preceding, you may use a reading from the Liturgy of the Hours, pages 14-31, or a lectionary reading of the day.)

Silent Reflection

Petitions

(Remember your intentions and those recommended by others at this time.)

Prayer

Mother of Perpetual Help, we your children come before you. You know the desire of your son who wishes to share with us the fullness of redemption. We ask you to assist us with your prayers. Mother of Christ, during the passion and death of your son, he gave you to us as a mother. You ask us to call you Mother of Perpetual Help. In confidence we present our needs to you and trust in your motherly care for us. Gather us together under your protection, and lead us one day to share with you and all the angels and saints the joys of heaven. Amen

Litany

Holy Mary,   **R. Pray for us.**
Mother of Jesus,
Tabernacle of the Holy Spirit,
Mother of the Poor,
Health of the Sick,
Consolation of the Suffering,
Mother of Perpetual Help,

Let us pray.

All powerful and merciful Lord, you give us the picture of the Mother of your son to venerate under the title of Our Mother of Perpetual Help. Graciously grant that in all the difficulties of our lives we may be assisted by the continuous protection of the Virgin Mary and obtain the reward of eternal redemption. You who live and reign forever and ever. Amen

(Now give thanks to God for all the blessings we have received through Mary's intercession in our lives. See page 21 for the Canticle of Mary. After the canticle, a hymn may be sung from your resources or from pages 78-80.)

Novena to
Our Lady of Guadalupe

A great sign appeared in heaven: a woman, clothed with the sun, with the moon under her feet and a crown of twelve stars on her head.*

* Revelation 12:1

Glorious Mother of the Redeemer, Compassionate Lady of Guadalupe! You are the glory of your people, the chosen vessel of God. In your loving concern for your people, you appeared to Juan Diego and revealed yourself as the mother of mercy and love. We come to you with our petitions: *(Here make your petitions for the novena.)* Hear our prayers, and show yourself a mother ever ready to assist us in our needs.

Who is this coming like the dawn, fair as the moon, bright as the sun! It is you, Holy Mother of our Savior. You are the Mystical Rose, the mother of the afflicted, the defender of the oppressed. Obtain for us a strong faith and ardent charity. Form us into a people eager to proclaim Jesus as our Lord. Hear us, beautiful Lady of Tepeyac, our Lady of Guadalupe.

Hail Mary....
V. Our Lady of Guadalupe,
R. Pray for us who have recourse to you.

Most glorious Virgin Mary, Mother of God, look with kindness upon us your children. Many are the difficulties that surround us in our Christian journey. In times of danger, be at our side with your protection. Help us to live our lives, faithful to the gospel of Jesus. Following your example, may we listen to the Word of God and surrender our lives to the action of the Holy Spirit. Pray for us, loving Mother of our Redeemer! Amen

Novena to Our Lady of the Miraculous Medal

Immaculate Virgin Mary, I unite myself to you under the title of Our Lady of the Miraculous Medal. I pray that this medal may be a sign of your protection and love for me. Keep me free from the evil of sin and surround me with your purity and humility. May this medal remind me of my devotion to you. Blessed Mother of my Savior, keep me close to you and grant that I may live and act according to the gospel of Jesus, your Son. Amen

The Memorare

Remember, O most gracious Virgin Mary, that never was it known that anyone who fled to your protection, implored your help, or sought your intercession was left unaided. Inspired with this confidence, I fly to you, O Virgin of Virgins, my Mother.

To you I come, before you I stand, sinful and sorrowful. O Mother of the Word Incarnate, despise not my petitions, but in your mercy, hear and answer me. Amen

V. O Mary conceived without sin,
R. Pray for us who have recourse to you.
(3 times)

Novena in Honor
of Our Sorrowful Mother

Feast Day: September 15

Near the cross of Jesus stood his mother, his mother's sister Mary, who was the wife of Cleophas, and Mary of Magdala. When Jesus saw the Mother, and the disciple, he said to the Mother, "Woman, this is your son." Then he said to the disciple, "There is your mother." And from that moment the disciple took her to his own home.

John 19:25-27

Mother of Sorrows, your heart was pierced by a sword of sorrow as you gazed upon the suffering and death of your beloved Jesus. I come before you with confidence that you will help me, for in your wounded, sorrowing heart I find a place of comfort and peace. I beg you, Mother of the Savior, to listen to my request. *(Pause here and make your request.)* For to whom shall I have recourse in my needs, if not to you Mother of compassion and love?

As you gazed upon your dying Jesus, you united your *fiat* to his cry of surrender: "Father, into your hands I surrender my spirit." I unite myself to you, Mother of mercy, and beg you to unite my sufferings with yours and offer them to Jesus. For you are our life, our sweetness, and our hope. Amen

The First Sorrow:
The Prophecy of Simeon

Simeon blessed them and said to Mary, his mother, "See him; he will be for the rise or fall of the multitudes of Israel. He shall stand as a sign of contradiction, while a sword will pierce your own soul. Then the secret thoughts of many may be brought to light."

Luke 2:34-35

Hail Mary....
V. Virgin Most Sorrowful,
R. Pray for us.

The Second Sorrow:
The Flight into Egypt

After the wise men had left, an angel of the Lord appeared in a dream to Joseph and said, "Get up, take the child and his mother and flee to Egypt, and stay there until I tell you. Herod will soon be looking for the child in order to kill him."

Joseph got up, took the child and his mother, and left that night for Egypt, where he stayed until the death of Herod.

Matthew 2:13-15

Hail Mary....
V. Virgin Most Sorrowful,
R. Pray for us.

The Third Sorrow:
The Loss of Jesus in the Temple

After the festival was over, they returned, but the boy Jesus remained in Jerusalem and his parents did not know it. On the first day of the journey they thought he was in the company and looked for him among their rela-

tives and friends. As they did not find him,
they went back to Jerusalem searching for him.

Luke 2:43-45

Hail Mary....
V. Virgin Most Sorrowful,
R. Pray for us.

The Fourth Sorrow:
Mary Meets Jesus on the Way to Calvary

A large crowd of people followed him; among
them were women beating their breast and
wailing for him, but Jesus turned to them and
said, "Women of Jerusalem, do not weep for
me, weep rather for yourselves and for your
children."

Luke 23:27-28

Hail Mary....
V. Virgin Most Sorrowful,
R. Pray for us.

The Fifth Sorrow:
Jesus Dies on the Cross

When Jesus saw the Mother, and the disciple, he said to the Mother, "Woman, this is your son." Then he said to the disciple, "There is your mother."

John 19:26-27

Hail Mary....
V. Virgin Most Sorrowful,
R. Pray for us.

The Sixth Sorrow:
Mary Receives the Dead Body
of Jesus in Her Arms

Joseph of Arimathea boldly went to Pilate and asked for the body of Jesus....Joseph took it down and wrapped it in the linen sheet he had bought.

Mark 15:43,46a

Hail Mary....
V. Virgin Most Sorrowful,
R. Pray for us.

The Seventh Sorrow:
Jesus Is Placed in the Tomb

He [Joseph] laid the body in a tomb which had been cut out of the rock and rolled a stone across the entrance to the tomb.

Mark 15:46b

Hail Mary....
V. Virgin Most Sorrowful,
R. Pray for us.

Let us pray.

Lord Jesus Christ, the prophecy of Simeon that a sword of sorrow would pierce the heart of your beloved Mother was fulfilled in her as she stood beneath the cross. May we who have commemorated with devotion her seven sorrows be united with her in offering our lives in loving surrender to your sacred passion. Amen

Rosary

∾∾

Basic Method

The complete rosary is composed of fifteen decades, divided into three parts, each part containing five decades. The first part consists of five joyful events in the lives of Jesus and Mary, the second part recalls five sorrowful events, and the third part considers five glorious events.

We begin by making the Sign of the Cross.

Then we say the Apostle's Creed, one Our Father, three Hail Marys (see page 41), and one Glory to the Father on the small chain. Then we recall the first mystery, say one Our Father, ten Hail Marys, and

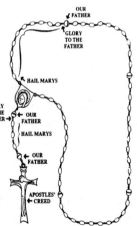

one Glory to the Father. This completes one decade. We say all the other decades in the same manner, meditating on a different mystery during each decade. At the end of the rosary, the prayer Hail, Holy Queen (see page 76) may be recited.

The mysteries of the rosary are scenes from the lives of Jesus and Mary. By meditating on these sublime truths, we come to a better understanding of our religion—the Incarnation of the Lord, the Redemption, and the Christian life, present and future.

Contemplative Method

Through the ages, many ways of praying the rosary developed. One method used during the Middle Ages was praying the rosary in a way that allowed for a contemplative centering on the mystery of Jesus living in Mary. The Hail Mary ends with "Blessed is the fruit of your womb." The second half of the prayer is not recited at this time. Instead, using the name of Jesus, it continues with a statement centering on the mystery of the decade, such as "Jesus, living in the womb of Mary." The traditional second half of the Hail Mary, which begins "Holy Mary Mother of God," is added at the end of the decade before the "Glory to the Father."

Praying the rosary in this manner slows down the pace and allows us to enter into the deep meaning of each mystery. It helps us to avoid distractions and inattentiveness in prayer.

The following is the method written out. In time you will be able to memorize the added statements allowing the prayer to flow from your heart.

Method

Once you have completed the introductory prayers, announce the first Mystery in the usual way. Pray the Lord's Prayer, then begin:

Hail Mary....Blessed is the fruit of your womb. Jesus, living in the womb of Mary.

Begin the second Hail Mary, and continue through the tenth. Then pray "Holy Mary, Mother of God..." etc., followed by the doxology. Then repeat the whole pattern through the remaining decades.

The Joyful Mysteries

1. Jesus, living in the womb of Mary. *(Remember to pray "Holy Mary, Mother of God....," but only once, at the end of the decade.)*
2. Jesus, who brought joy to Elizabeth.
3. Jesus, who was born in a stable.
4. Jesus, who was recognized by Anna and Simeon.
5. Jesus, who was found in the Temple.

The Sorrowful Mysteries

1. Jesus, suffering alone in agony.
2. Jesus, struck and insulted by the soldiers.
3. Jesus, carrying your cross in pain and suffering.
4. Jesus, nailed to a cross.
5. Jesus, pierced by a lance.

The Glorious Mysteries

1. Jesus, who rose from the grave.
2. Jesus, who ascended into heaven.
3. Jesus, who sends the Holy Spirit upon us.
4. Jesus, who assumed Mary into heaven.
5. Jesus, who crowned Mary queen of the universe.

Scriptural Meditations of the Rosary

The Joyful Mysteries
Mondays and Thursdays

1. THE ANNUNCIATION OF OUR LORD

But the angel said, "Do not fear, Mary, for God has looked kindly on you. You shall conceive and bear a son and you shall call him Jesus. He will be great and shall rightly be called Son of the Most High."

Luke 1:30-32

2. THE VISITATION

"You are most blessed among women and blessed is the fruit of your womb!...Blessed are you who believed that the Lord's word would come true!"

Luke 1:42,45

3. THE NATIVITY OF JESUS

They were in Bethlehem when the time came for her to have her child, and she gave birth to a son, her firstborn. She wrapped him in swaddling clothes and laid him in the manger, because there was no place for them in the [inn].

Luke 2:6-7

4. THE PRESENTATION IN THE TEMPLE

When the day came for the purification according to the law of Moses, they brought the baby up to Jerusalem to present him to the Lord.

Luke 2:22

5. THE FINDING IN THE TEMPLE

After three days they found him in the Temple, sitting among the teachers, listening to them and asking questions.

Luke 2:46

The Sorrowful Mysteries

Tuesdays and Fridays

1. THE AGONY IN THE GARDEN

Jesus came with them to a place called Gethsemane, and he said to his disciples, "Sit here while I go over to pray."…He went a little farther and fell to the ground, with his face touching the earth, and prayed, "Father if it is possible, take this cup away from me. Yet not what I want, but what you want."

Matthew 26:36,39

2. *THE SCOURGING AT THE PILLAR*

All the people answered, "Let his blood be upon us and upon our children."

Then Pilate set Barabbas free, but had Jesus scourged, and handed him over to be crucified.

Matthew 27:25-26

3. *THE CROWNING WITH THORNS*

They stripped him and dressed him in a purple military cloak. Then, twisting a crown of thorns, they forced it onto his head, and placed a reed in his right hand. They knelt before Jesus and mocked him, saying, "Long life to the King of the Jews!"

Matthew 27:28-29

4. *THE CARRYING OF THE CROSS*

Bearing his own cross, Jesus went out of the city to what is called the Place of the Skull, in Hebrew: *Golgotha.* There he was crucified and with him two others, one on either side, and Jesus was in the middle.

John 19:17-18

5. THE CRUCIFIXION AND DEATH

The sun was hidden and darkness came over the whole land until mid-afternoon; and at that time the curtain of the Sanctuary was torn in two. Then Jesus gave a loud cry, "Father, into your hands, I commend my spirit." And saying that, he gave up his spirit.

Luke 23:45-46

The Glorious Mysteries

1. THE RESURRECTION OF OUR LORD

The Angel said to the women, "Do not be afraid, for I know that you are looking for Jesus who was crucified. He is not here, for he is risen as he said. Come, see the place where they laid him."

Matthew 28:5-6

2. THE ASCENSION INTO HEAVEN

Jesus led them almost as far as Bethany; then he lifted up his hands and blessed them. And as he blessed them, he withdrew (and was taken to heaven. They worshipped him).

Luke 24:50-51

3. THE DESCENT OF THE HOLY SPIRIT

Suddenly out of the sky came a sound like a strong rushing wind and it filled the whole house where they were sitting. There appeared tongues as if of fire which parted and came to rest upon each one of them. All were filled with Holy Spirit.

Acts 2:2-4

4. THE ASSUMPTION OF MARY

"My daughter, may the Most High God bless you more than all women on earth.

And blessed be the Lord God, the Creator of heaven and earth."

Judith 13:18

5. THE CORONATION OF MARY

A great sign appeared in heaven: a woman, clothed with the sun, with the moon under her feet and a crown of twelve stars on her head.

Revelation 12:1

Prayer after the Rosary

O God, whose only-begotten Son, by his life, death, and resurrection, has purchased for us the rewards of eternal life, grant, we beseech you, that we who meditate upon these mysteries of the most holy rosary of the Blessed Virgin Mary, may imitate what they contain and obtain what they promise. We ask this through Christ our Lord. Amen

Prayers to the Blessed Virgin Mary

❧

Prayer to Our Lady of Mount Carmel

O beautiful flower of Carmel, most fruitful vine, splendor of heaven, holy and singular, who brought forth the Son of God, still ever remaining a pure virgin, assist me in this necessity. O Star of the Sea, help and protect me. Show me that you are my Mother. Patroness of all who wear the scapular, pray for us! Hope of all who die wearing the scapular, pray for us! O sweet heart of Mary, be our salvation. Amen

Prayer to Our Lady of Czestochowa

Holy Mother of Czestochowa, you are full of grace, goodness and mercy. I consecrate to you all my thoughts, words and actions—my soul and body. I beseech your blessings and especially prayers for my salvation.

Today, I consecrate myself to you, good Mother, totally—with body and soul, amid joy and sufferings, to obtain for myself and others your blessings on this earth and eternal life in heaven. Amen

Hail, Holy Queen
(Salve Regina)

Hail, holy queen, mother of mercy, our life, our sweetness, and our hope. To you we cry, poor banished children of Eve; to you we send up our sighs, mourning and weeping in this valley of tears. Turn then, O most gracious advocate, your eyes of mercy toward us, and after this our exile, show unto us the blessed fruit of your womb, Jesus. O clement, O loving, O sweet virgin Mary.

Prayer to Our Lady, Help of Christians

Most holy and Immaculate Virgin Mary, our tender mother and mighty help of Christians, we dedicate ourselves completely to your dear love and holy service. We dedicate to you our minds and our thoughts, our hearts and all our affections, our bodies and our senses and all our strength. We promise to be ever willing to labor for the greater glory of God and the salvation of souls.

Grant to us, O Mary, Help of Christians, to be gathered under your maternal protection. May the thought of the love you bear toward your devoted sons and daughters be a great source of strength for us and make us victors over the enemies of our salvation, both in life and in death, so that we may come to stand with you in the beauty of paradise. Amen

Hymns

Hail, Holy Queen Enthroned Above

Hail! holy Queen enthroned above,
    O Maria!
Hail, Queen of mercy and of love,
    O Maria!

Refrain: Triumph all ye Cherubim,
Sing with us, ye Seraphim,
Heav'n and earth resound the hymn:
Salve, salve, salve, Regina!
Our life, our sweetness here below,
    O Maria!
Our hope in sorrow and in woe, O Maria!
(Refrain)

Text: *Salve, Regina Coelitum,* anon., Latin, c. 1080, verses 1,2,5 and refrain, tr. by anon., c. 1884, alt.; verses 3,4,6, para. by editors, 1980.

Tune: Melchior Ludwig Herold's *Choralmelodien zum Heiligen Gesänge,* 1808, and later in Siona, 1832.

Salve, Regina Coelitum 8.4.8.4 with refrain.

Immaculate Mary

Immaculate Mary, your praises we sing;
You reign now with Jesus, our Savior and
King.

Refrain: Ave, Ave, Ave, Maria! Ave, Ave,
Maria!

In heaven the blessed your glory proclaim;
On earth we, your children, invoke your
fair name.
(Refrain)

We pray for the Church, our true mother on
earth,
And ask you to watch o'er the land of our
birth.
(Refrain)

Text: Anon., in *Parochial Hymn Book,* Boston, 1897, rev. version of
"Hail, Virgin of Virgins," by Jeremiah Cummings, 1814-1866, in his
Songs for Catholic Schools, 1860, alt.

Tune: Trad. Pyrenean melody.

Lourdes (Massabielle) 11 11 with refrain.

Queen of Heaven

(Prayer during the Easter season instead of the Angelus)

V. Queen of heaven, rejoice, alleluia.

R. The Son whom you were privileged to bear, alleluia,

V. Has risen as he said, alleluia.

R. Pray to God for us, alleluia.

V. Rejoice and be glad, Virgin Mary, alleluia.

R. For the Lord has truly risen, alleluia.

V. Let us pray:

All: O God, by the Resurrection of your Son, our Lord Jesus Christ, you brought joy to the world. Grant that through the intercession of the Virgin Mary, his Mother, we may attain the joy of eternal life. We ask this through Christ our Lord. Amen